CHAKRAS FOR

BEGINNERS

Discover the Secrets to Opening Your Chakras For Self-Healing, Positive Energies and Mind Expansion

Noah Grayton

Published By:

DANA PUBLISHING

P.O. Box 1801

Mentor, Ohio 44060

Legal & Disclaimer

as and when needed. Where appropriate and/or necessary, you must consult a professional (including but not limited to your doctor, attorney, financial advisor or such other professional advisor) before using any of the suggested remedies, techniques, or information in this book.

Upon using the contents and information contained in this book, you agree to hold harmless the Author from and against any damages, costs, and expenses, including any legal fees potentially resulting from the application of any of the information provided by this book. This disclaimer applies to any loss, damages or injury caused by the use and application, whether directly or indirectly, of any advice or information presented, whether for breach of contract, tort, negligence, personal injury, criminal intent, or under any other cause of action.

You agree to accept all risks of using the information presented inside this book.

You agree that by continuing to read this book, where appropriate and/or necessary, you shall consult a professional (including but not limited to your doctor, attorney, or financial advisor or such other advisor as needed) before using any of the suggested remedies, techniques, or information in this book.

Table of Contents

Chakras Introduction

The Chakras are vital energy centers found inside of your body and are in charge of regulating all of the processes that occur inside energetically. This can include organ functions, your emotions and even how well the immune system works.

For the most part, there are 7 main chakras and they are going to be positioned all throughout the body. Some people believe that there are some lesser chakras, but for now we are going to focus on some of the more familiar ones and how they are going to work in your body. These main chakras are going to be found from the base of the spine all the way up to the head and each one will have its own vibration, which is often shown with a specific color that comes with the chakra.

Each of the chakras works on a different part of the body. For example, the first chakra is going to be in charge of helping you to feel connections with the other people around you while the crown chakra opens you up to some of the things that happen in the spiritual world. All of the chakras are important, and they even work together, even though they may seem to work on such different parts of the body. When one of the chakras is not working properly, it can start to affect how the other chakras are going to work. And if you don't take the time to give the chakras the healing that they need, you are going to start noticing that many of the chakras will start to fail.

In addition, there are several ways that things can go wrong with the chakras. Many times when there are issues, it is because the chakras are closed off and aren't able to let in some of the energy that is needed. For example, when the heart chakra is closed off, you may not be able to experience emotions and you may be seen as cold hearted to other people. In addition, you may find that the heart chakra, or any of the other chakras, could be too opened, which could result in you feeling too many emotions and always being a wreck from these emotions.

It is important that you work on keeping the chakras balanced as much as possible. In our modern world, this can seem like something that is almost impossible to work on. You are already overworked, stressed out, and so much more, so how much sense does it make to keep the chakras in balance if everything in your life is already working against you? It does take a little bit of dedication and hard work, but with some persistence, you are able to make your chakras as strong as possible.

Keys to Chakra Healing

As mentioned, it is really important for you to work on healing the chakras as much as you can. When the chakras are opened just the right amount, but not too much, you are able to have a life that is <u>well balanced</u> and much happier than before. This can take some times and you will have to learn how to do this on your own. Each person finds their own way to getting the chakra healing that they are looking for.

With that being said, there are a few keys to chakra healing that anyone is able to work with in order to get the chakras to feel better and to be back on track. Some of the keys to chakra healing that you can consider include:

- **Chakra balancing: if you are curious as to what a healthy chakra is going to look like, you need to work on balancing the chakras. The foundation to having a healthy system is to balance and open up the chakras. This allows them to create what is known as a harmonious and sustainable flow of energy throughout the body.**

- **Opening up the chakras: often the biggest issue that you are dealing with when it comes to your chakras is that they are closed up, so there are a number of practices that will work to open up the chakras. These are some of the more traditional schools of thought that are found with the Eastern spirituality, but this is a good one to use to help out with your chakras.**

- **Healing techniques for the chakras: some of the healing techniques that are available today for the chakras are going to be created by people who come from a wide variety of fields. They are** going to include options from fields like psychology, fitness, holistic medicine, and healing, which can make them so much more powerful than before.

Chapter 1: What are the Chakras?

If you've never heard of a Chakra, then you've come to the right place to start your journey. Some people avoid talking about things like this, because they're "too spiritual" or "too metaphysical." That being said, if you're willing to open up and try for yourself, you will discover that the more you work with your chakras, the more your life will change for the better. In short, the Chakras are energy focuses along the primary meridian of the body, and they are used to help you focus different parts of your energy into positive use, which can help you to accomplish more in your life than you ever have before.

The word "chakra" comes from old Sanskrit. The term means "wheel" or "round," and is, for the most part, used to reference particular energy focuses along the body's center line. By and large, there are seven primary chakra focuses. The first time that we see any mention of Chakras is from the Vedas, which structure the Hindu scriptures. There are additional mentions of energy focuses from other traditions, for example, in Chinese acupressure texts. Most spiritual frameworks that nurture the mind will also talk about energy points as well, because they play a vital role in helping the body to heal and thrive appropriately. The energy is regularly depicted as climbing from the Root Chakra to the Crown Chakra, and then up into the heavens. Energy also enters the body through the Crown Chakra, descends to the Root Chakra, and continues into the earth.

The First Chakra is located between the genitals and the anus, and is called the Root Chakra, and is in association with Earth, security, establishment, and fundamental rootedness. It is additionally at times considered a position of possibility and beginnings.

The Second Chakra, which is sometimes called the sacral chakra, is placed at the front of the body, in the area that many refer to as "the crotch", and is connected with sexuality, organization (both non-sentimental and sentimental), and imagination. It is considered analogous to the Chinese Yin and Yang symbol, where the energies of both genders (male and female) come together into a whole.

The Third Chakra is located in the solar plexus, just beneath the rib cage. It is the focus for a person's will. We extend our will out into the world through this chakra, and it plays a strong role in manifesting our goals in reality.

The Fourth Chakra is located in the center of the chest, near the heart, and is associated with love and affection. In some traditions, it is believed that the heart chakra has two aspects: is considered male and governs one's feelings for others; the other is considered female and relates to one's feelings for oneself.

The Fifth Chakra is located in the throat, and controls self-expression and your ability to speak your heart and your mind. This is the spot of thoughts, ideas, and general articulation, and it is also the place where you find truth that is specific to you and your particular life and needs.

The Sixth Chakra is at the position of the third eye, and is identified with "second sight." This chakra is regularly connected with psychic capacities of different sorts, and many believe that everyone has the capability of unlocking this Chakra, no matter what sort of abilities you feel like you may or may not have.

The Seventh Chakra is the crown chakra, spotted at the highest point of the head. It is associated with the assimilation of new knowledge and the ability to reach into the heavens. It is important to understand the Crown Chakra, because it helps you to pull everything that you are learning together under one banner.

It is vital to learn why we would use these, what the profits are of doing so, and how we can utilize them in order to fully get a hold on ourselves and how we are meant to live our lives. Here are some additional thoughts on the Chakras, so that you can have a better understanding of them and how they work.

Numerous healing ideologies use chakras to evaluate and look over an individual and to determine precisely what work ought to be carried out on that individual. The chakras can additionally be utilized as a place to discover different sorts of healing, while also taking a close look at exactly what type of damage may have already been done.

Chakra work gives a premise to specialists so that they can put together the puzzle of the whole person and their particular problems. By sensing and working with an individual's chakras, an expert will achieve a greater understanding of any issues their patient is struggling with. This also provides a starting point on the journey to essential healing.

Consider that when it comes to chakras there are a variety of traditions in existence, and some may include other chakras besides those mentioned here. One tradition may work better for you, but that doesn't mean it's better for others. This is simply due to the fact that all people are different and live different lives, so what may work for some will not work for others.

These chakras, or energy focuses, work as pumps or valves, directing the stream of energy through our energy framework. The care of the chakras reflects choices we make concerning how we decide to react to conditions throughout our life. We open and close these valves when we choose what to think, and what to feel, and through which perceptual channel we decide to encounter our general surroundings.

The chakras are not physical. They are parts of the consciousness in the same way that the emanations are parts of cognizance. The chakras are denser than the specific qualities that they represent and heal, yet not as dense as the physical body. They connect with the physical body through two significant vehicles; the endocrine framework and the sensory system. Each of the seven chakras is connected with one of the seven endocrine organs, and, additionally, with a gathering of nerves called a plexus. Hence, every chakra is connected with specific parts of the body, and specific capacities inside the body are controlled by the plexus and the endocrine organ connected with that chakra.

The greater part of your faculties, your consciousness, the majority of your observations, and all that you may encounter in life, could be separated into seven classes. Every class could be connected with a specific chakra. Accordingly, the chakras speak to specific parts of your physical body, as well as specific parts of your mind.

When you feel pressure in your mind, you feel it in the chakra connected with the stress, and you feel it in the physical part of the body that is also connected to the stress. Where you feel the anxiety depends on why you feel the anxiety. The pressure in the chakra is identified by the nerves of the plexus connected with that chakra, and transmitted to the parts of the body controlled by that same plexus. At a certain point, the individual starts to notice physical pain as well.

These manifestations help us to figure out exactly what is going on in our mind and body, and the figurative criticalness of the manifestation becomes clear when we start to see them for ourselves.

The manifestation served to convey to the individual through their body what they had been doing to themselves in their emotional and mental mind. When someone finally accepts what is possible in their life, then they are able to start, as well as see the healing, as indicated by whatever the individual permits themselves to accept is conceivable.

We think everything is conceivable. We accept that anything can be fixed and healed. It's simply a matter of how to do it. Understanding the chakras permits you to comprehend the relationship between your body and your mind, and to subsequently see your body as a guide of your awareness. It provides you with a superior understanding of yourself and those around you. It can help you to get started with the healing that you deserve, and it can help you to find ways to live the life that you've always wanted to live.

Chapter 2: Chakra history

While the chakras are part of an ancient tradition, they are starting to make a re-appearance again. There are many new interpretations of their meaning and their functions, and sometimes it is easy to get confused since there are so many ways to think about these chakras. While the popularity is starting to make the chakras more of a word that people recognize, there are a lot of times when this information is going to be erroneous, conflicting, and even confusing. Before you work on making the chakras a part of your life, it is important to understand some of the history that comes with these chakras and can better explain how they should be used.

The Vedas are some of the oldest written tradition from the area of India and it was recorded from the oral tradition of the upper caste Brahmins. The original meaning of this word of chakra is "wheel" which refers to the chariot wheels that were used by the rulers of that time. The word has also been used in these texts as a metaphor for the sun, which is able to traverse the world just like a triumphant chariot and will denote the eternal wheel of time, which also represents balance and order, just like the idea of the wheel and what the chakras are going to focus on.

The birth of the chakras was said to herald in a brand new age, and they were often described as being preceded by a disk of light, such as the halo of Christ, but there was a spinning disk that was in front of them. It is also said that Vishnu, the god, descended to Earth, carrying the charka, a club, a conch shell, and a lotus flower.

In these texts, there are also some mentions of the chakras being like a psychic center of consciousness in several different versions of this text including the Yoga Sutras of Patanjali and the Yoga Upanishads. The implied goal of Yoga was to rise above nature and the world that you are living in, in order to find the realization of a pure consciousness, one that was free from any fluctuations that came in with the emotions and the mind. Yet the word of yoga stands for yoke or union, so the realization that happens in between consciousness and realizations must ultimately reintegrate with nature to get a higher synthesis.

So, since the idea of yoga and the chakras arose inside of the same tradition, the Tantric tradition, it is no wonder that they are often associated together. As we will discuss later on, you will be able to find that yoga is one of the ways that you will be able to bring the chakras into line because they were both developed in the same traditions and both can be used at the same time.

In the traditional ideas of chakras, there are seven of the basic ones and they are all going to exist inside of your body. Through modern physiology, it is easy to see that the seven chakras are going to correspond exactly to the main nerve ganglia inside of the body, which all come from the spinal column. While many people assume that these chakras have nothing to do with them any longer, the chakras were well placed, put into specific parts of the body where nerves are located and where different parts can influence how the rest of the body is going to react. It is interesting that the chakras were able to develop based on these thoughts, even before all of the nerves and pressure points would have been realized.

In addition to the main seven chakras that most people concentrate on, there are a few minor chakras that are mentioned inside of the ancient tasks. For example, there is the soma chakra which you will be able to find right above the third eye chakra and then there is the Ananda Kanda lotus, which is going to be near the heart chakra, plus some more options based on how deep into the ancient texts that you choose to go.

Many people assume that the chakras are an ancient idea that you shouldn't pay any attention to. They figure that the chakras have nothing to do with how they live their modern life and they may assume it was all a bunch of spirituality that is just made up. But in reality, you will find that in modern times, the chakras are more important compared to any other time. We need to understand how easy we can get out of balance. We are always running around, always stressed out and worried, and often we have trouble with some of our own relationships. Chakras are able to get these back in line better than anything else.

People who practice balancing their chakras are often going to be so much healthier and happier, and better able to get through the day, compared to others who don't even believe in the chakras and just keep going through all of the bad things that are in their lives. It is definitely worth your time to ensure that you are able to get the great life that you would like without all the issues.

Chakras and Science

For a long time, science was unable, or unwilling, to explore the chakras and chakra healing. While there is still limited Western science "backing up" the chakra energy centers, it is clear that your body functions thanks to the systems or energetic impulses inside it. Everything you do and think is controlled by this system of energy, which Western science has proven time and time again. Simply looking at the brain's electrical pulses shows how energy rules this vital organ. Before modern science, the chakras were a good method for describing how the body functioned or was even able to function. Now, science may have labeled these properties something different or still cannot explain why certain things in your body works the way they do, but there are some things that this ancient science and today's modern understanding do agree on.

The first thing that science and the charkas agree on is that your body is made up of energy, and so is everything else around you. In fact, nothing around you is actually a solid piece of reality; it is simply a collection of energy particles deciding to hold together for a short time. Think about a chair. It may appear solid and sturdy to you; however, at its most basic level, it is just a combination of atoms. Atoms are not solid or static items. Inside these atoms are even smaller particles that are constantly moving and adjusting. Those particles are not solid, either. These particles inside the atom are called subatomic particles and are the electrons, neutrons, and protons. The neutrons and protons huddle together at the center of the atom, while the electrons race around on the outside. These move so quickly that scientists cannot determine where an electron is exactly at from one instance to the next.

In addition to being made up of energy and racing electrons and huddling subatomic particles, an atom is mostly made up of space. In fact, it is estimated that each atom is 99.99% space. This space is what allows for all this movement. And this information is true, not just about your chair, but about everything around you and you yourself! Your body and mind are always moving and changing, much more subtle than you may ever feel or know. Nothing in this world exists without energy.

Science now is able to understand and prove this, but religions have understood for thousands of years the powerful role energy plays in your life. Chakras, tai chi, yoga, QiGong, and reiki are all examples of spiritual practices that deal with moving your energy. And the purpose of this movement is to help your body and your existence find a state of well-being and harmony. These ancient religions understand that we are influenced by and can similarly influence back, this transference and movement of energy through your actions, including your thoughts. This is because your brain is also moving and thoughts are your reality.

Science has begun to explain some of this movement and transference. For example, even when you are sleeping, your body is moving energy around. According to science, this happens mainly through your neurons and nerve pathways. In the ancient sciences and spirituality, it was explained through the chakras and the nadis. No matter what you are consciously or unconsciously doing, your body is a course of flowing energy. This includes digesting your food, thinking, moving your limbs, breathing, and even healing yourself.

The signals the nervous system transmits go from the brain to the body and from the body back to the brain. There are receptors all along the length of your body and all throughout, so you can coordinate your actions with your needs and wants. Again, this includes both the conscious and unconscious actions your body takes. When you lift your arm, you are making use of your nervous system and sending energy to your arm to lift it up. When you eat something, your body begins a series of energetic processes to digest, absorb, and remove the waste of that food. These are examples of voluntary and involuntary actions that require energy and communication between receptors and your brain.

In ancient religions, there are many ways to move this energy so it can continue to support the proper functioning of your body. Things like yoga poses, meditation, and breathing practices are all ways to move energy and restore harmonious balance in your life. Chakra healing and balancing is another method, and this often includes a combination of various techniques to move your energy. Both quantum mechanics and "traditional" science suggest that focusing on your thoughts can make a large difference in your overall well-being. For example, visualization techniques have been successfully used to help improve mental functioning and prevent deterioration of the brain in patients that suffered negative side effects from a stroke. Focusing on the chakras and the movement of energy through the nadis is a great method, used for thousands of years and supported through modern science, for bringing peace and well-being to your life. It may be called something different, but it is really similar to one another.

Your energetic body, made up of these subtle energetic impulses, is best revealed in your heart and brain. Your brain is probably one of the best places to "look" to see how powerful energy is at work in your body. In your brain alone, there are more than one hundred billion "wires" that conduct energetic impulses. These impulses are actually charged up ions coursing through your body, making sure your heart is pumping and your muscles are moving. They are biological pathways that are critical to your proper functioning. Observing the electricity of the brain is a great way to understand how your body is made up of energy.

In addition to the energy living inside of you, there is energy surrounding your body, too. It is often hard to comprehend when you see and feel the boundary of skin and know the solidity of bones, but there is an electromagnetic field surrounding your body. This has a certain frequency. This can seem like New Age and ancient "non-sense" until you realize that scientist uses this understanding when they measure these frequencies with machines like an MRI or ECG machine. A change in energy in a certain location tells them something is out of balance, and they can see it through the image these machines produce.

Psychology is another modern scientific field that examines the mind and why we think and behave in certain ways. According to Psychology Today, every person is a physical embodiment of an energetic field. The chakras go further to explain that there are centers in the body for this energy to flow through. These movements control your emotions, organs, and immune system, among other things. When all things are flowing as they should, you are balanced spiritually, physically, emotionally, and mentally. That is why your chakras are so important to your overall well-being.

On the contrary, if there is a blockage in your energy, you become ill. This is seen in scientific tests such as a CT scan or an MRI. A tumor appears like a black spot in an otherwise energetic and moving system. It is blocking your energy in that place and you are not well. Other times, it manifests in your mental ability. An energy block can cause mental illness such as anxiety, depression, or more. Practicing ways to clear and move your energy is a powerful tool. A recent study showed that participants that suffered from a stroke saw marked improvements in the health of their brain when they spent time visualizing lifting a limb that was paralyzed during the stroke. The stroke damaged a part of their brain that sends the energetic information to that limb to move but visualizing it moving helped strengthen the brain tissue around that damaged area so the deterioration did not spread. This is just one modern scientific example of how an ancient tradition of moving energy with your thoughts can cause significant improvement to your physical well-being.

Your mental state is known to impact your physical body. We see this most in the correlation between stress and your health. Stress is an emotional and mental state, but when it is too prevalent, it causes a cascade of physical ailments along with it. According to the National Institute of Health, stress is an imbalance in your life. This imbalance, real or perceived, triggers the body to try to find and restore balance. These situations cause stress release hormones that are incredibly powerful and that lead to the feeling of anxiety and stimulation. Contemporary science lists stress as a major factor in numerous illnesses, such as cancer and mental illness. Stress costs millions of dollars a year in medical expenses. This is a constant discussion in modern science and most doctors and scientists agree that reducing stress is vital in supporting your overall health.

In addition, contemporary science and medicine are beginning to understand and promote healthy mental health alongside physical health. It has become more and more obvious that a person's mental state is as important, if not more so, than their physical body in restoring balance in their overall health. Good treatment not only includes treating the physical body but the mental and spiritual as well. According to the National Institute of Health, most books dealing with the spiritual or mental treatment of an individual is more spiritual in nature, keeping the topic foreign to most physicians, but Western medicine must begin to create a more comprehensive model to treat the gross and subtle bodies of a person. This means Western science needs to continue their understanding of how the energy in the mind and spirit connect to the physical body as they treat patients.

Almost a century ago, in the West, Sir William Osler documented a case where a patient suffered from an asthma attack after smelling an artificial rose. This posed a curious question that science, at the time, could not explain. There was no physical reason that this should have happened. Dr. Robert Adler, in 1975, offered an explanation to this question; a person's thoughts can control their immune system. Sir William Osler was curious about why mammals were able to have controlled immune responses, and Dr. Adler was finally able to explain it. In his experiments, Dr. Adler was able to prove that a person's emotions and thoughts could create significant changes in their physical body and immune system.

Before these findings, Western science thought each body system worked independently of one another. The foundation of our modern science considered your immune system to not be impacted by your emotional or mental state. Dr. Adler proved this is not the case. His findings showed that, indeed, your entire body works together impacting each part to find balance or homeostasis. It was also his findings that first explained that stress negatively impacts your physical well-being.

You can finally begin to see more traditional, Western doctors embracing the understanding that your mental state is a major impact on your physical body, but it is something that Eastern traditions have known for thousands of years. Ancient science knew that energy is life and an imbalance in this energy, in any form, disrupts your physical existence. Energy needs to flow freely, and one of the best ways you can do this is by taking certain actions to find this balance. You can use meditation, visualization, eating certain foods, performing certain physical actions, etc. to move this life force, or vital energy, through your body and find balance. When you can keep these hubs or channels of energy clear, like keeping plaque out of your arteries for proper blood flow, you can live a more healthy and harmonious life. Unfortunately, many Western cultures do not focus on this integrated approach. This results in dormant, inactive, or blocked energy centers. This leads to a disruption in the flow of energy, and ultimately, to disease and imbalance.

Chapter 3: Chakras and consciousness

Chakras are often referred to as the centers of consciousness. Often, what comes out of your mouth will dictate where your emotions and how your days and life will go. This state will tie in with your ability and capacity to think before speaking and acting.

It is said that the best ways to activate your chakra are yoga and meditation. Both practices can bring you to a higher state of consciousness and keep the mind clear, focused, and grounded.

Evolving Chakras

Often, you will see pictures of color auras forming in a vertical line from a figure's spine to the top of its head. That line shows where the seven main chakra points are located. All your thoughts and emotions are inside its appropriate points. Your consciousness and focus are the two main factors that deal with the kind of energy you currently have and how it flows or doesn't flow.

When you lose focus and your thoughts become unclear and disorganized, your flow is weakened. However, it is still up to **you** and **only** you to determine how this energy flows, because it is up to **you** to decide how you will deal with the negativities of others and your surroundings. Being physically ill and/or in pain or discomfort also takes a severe toll on your overall energy, even sometimes causing you to lose it altogether, albeit for a short period of time.

The stronger your energy flow, the more aware you are and the more spiritually inclined and connected you will be.

The following paragraphs will explain the seven levels of consciousness, tying in with each main chakra point.

The First Tier of Consciousness: Root Chakra

Humans, so far, have the most sophisticated levels and understanding of consciousness. However, keep in mind that despite your level of spiritually inclination or connection, you are still a human being dependent on the basic necessities such as food, shelter, water, and adequate rest for survival.

Past feelings, memories, and lessons learned from past events are stored inside the root chakra. While it is still okay to feel sadness or pain, the root chakra becomes stronger if you learn lessons from past mistakes and learn to deal with past tragedies or other painful memories in a constructive manner.

Allowing these past hardships to define your life will hinder your improvement in the present and the future, so much so that it can cause long-term health problems down the road.

To keep this chakra balanced, chant a mantra to yourself. For example, reassure yourself that you are strong and protected. Meditation is also important. Try to imagine yourself connected, or rooted and firmly grounded, to the Earth, hence the name "root" chakra.

Do **not** rely exclusively on gemstones for this chakra, or any of the other chakras. It's important to get your healthy nutrients in, too. For this chakra, carrots, beets, potatoes and any other vegetable that grows out of the ground are your best bet. Also, be sure to pay attention to proteins, such as eggs and legumes. If you can handle spicy foods, hot peppers are also highly beneficial.

The Second Tier of Consciousness: Sacral Chakra

Here is where you develop your own sense of self, in part with the choices you in what and with whom you surround yourself. You develop communication skills and learn to enhance them properly. With this development of your own identity, you are not only shaping yourself but also how you interact and connect with other humans, and the kinds of romantic, familial and friendly relationships you build with them.

To balance the sacral, reassure yourself that you are creative and that you love and are passionate about life. When you meditate, rest your hand on the lower abdomen and picture an orange light and imagine it surrounding you, freeing you from worry and self-critical feelings. The more conscious the sacral, the more dedicated you are to your realistic goals, without anything to stop you from achieving them, albeit by positive, non-hurtful means. The right food would be oranges, strawberries, melons, vanilla, honey, and cinnamon.

The Third Tier of Consciousness: The Solar Plexus Chakra

In this state, you already have your own identity shaped will now develop your very own way of articulation, although some of it may be influenced by the methods of speaking from others, especially from those that live in close proximity to you. It also allows you to learn from and correct your own mistakes so they don't carry over to the rest of your life. In its strongest form, you have full control and grasp of your own life, without having to rely on **anyone else** to help shape it for you. You have the complete freedom and street-smarts to live your life and plan your future on YOUR own terms.

To prevent this chakra from blockage, use such mantras as "I control my own destiny" and picture a yellow/gold aura around you.

During meditation, fix your eyes on the flame of a fireplace or a candle and imagine a flame igniting inside you, giving you your own strength. Your grains and dairies are most essential for awakening and strengthening the navel chakra.

The Fourth Tier of Consciousness: The Heart Chakra

This stage allows you to fully see the true joy and beauty in life, particularly in the simplest and smallest things. It also allows you to give love and compassion fully and experience both in return. Negative feelings are removed from your mind and body when this stage is at its peak, and you also focus much less on materialistic things and more on the deep meanings of life.

For mantras, reassure yourself that you love all the world and that you, in return, are loved. Your meditation sessions should consist of focusing on someone you love and assuring yourself that you will be happy and healthy, and in return wish everyone you love the same sentiments. Also learn to look past not only your own mistakes and flaws but the mistakes and flaws of others, too.

Foods that are essential for heart health are mostly the green vegetables, especially those with leaves and herbs.

The Fifth Tier of Consciousness: The Throat Chakra

In its strongest stage, your communication skills and ability to vocally express your emotions openly and without worries are at their peak. It also shows that you have already established the full ability and confidence to think for yourself and not be swayed by the opinions of others. However, keep in mind that it is never okay to express yourself in a mean-spirited, bullying, and abusive way.

To keep this chakra healthy, drink herbal teas such as lemongrass and fruit juices particularly in the citrus family. During meditation, assure yourself by repeating mantras related to living life only on your own terms.

The Sixth Tier of Consciousness: The Third Eye Chakra

This stage allows you to experience senses beyond the basic five of smell, taste, touch, hearing, and sight. You will also have full understanding of what it means to be truly connected to the universe. However, take care that you do not let your ego get in the way, overinflate, or become grandiose. These kinds of actions can lead to headaches and inability to understand others and their feelings. Moreover, you may become very judgmental rather than a supportive listener.

At meditation, picture a ball of indigo blue around you. The best foods to keep this chakra working properly are found in the blue/purple families, such as eggplant, blueberries, and anything containing sage, rosemary, and lavender. Also, keep a supply of walnuts handy.

The Seventh Tier of Consciousness: The Crown Chakra

Here, you are at your highest consciousness level, where you develop wisdom from past mistakes and even past accolades. However, keep in mind that life itself is a learning process and experience. To grow from this experience is to remember that we are all one and connected to the whole universe.

At the seventh tier, you also become deeply connected in the spiritual sense, and the higher power is by your side. Actually becoming one with the higher power, however, is a near-impossible feat, as it is very rare that one reaches this level of consciousness and mindfulness, but you are still completely aware and mindful when you do reach this stage.

No mantras are needed here, just silence to ensure your mind is at its clearest. Close your eyes and imagine a white light fully radiating inside of you.

Drink plenty of water and avoid any and all processed foods to keep this chakra open and working to its fullest potential. Once you are able to reach this stage, you are completely at peace and quietude.

Chapter 4: The seven chakras

You would often hear the word "chakra" when you are speaking with a spiritual healer, chiropractor, acupuncturist, or a yoga teacher. But, it's a word that's not commonly used in this modern world. In fact, the word "chakra" does not appeal to a lot of people because it sounds too "hippie" or "new agey".

Many people think that these chakras are not real and that they do not exist. But, chakras are real and they have a huge impact in your life, whether you believe in them or not. They influence the level of your energy. They also govern your emotions, your health, and even the quality of your life and relationships.

But, what are chakras? Where are they located and why should you care about them?

Chakras are energy centers or fields of the body. These energy fields, primarily operate on your spirit or non-physical body, but they do correlate with areas of the physical body.

The chakras are wheels that move the energy up and down the body as they spin. They are connected to specific organs and glands in the body and they are responsible for the distribution of the life energy called "chi/qi" or "prana".

The chakras are the foundation of your energy ecosystem. Problems or deficiencies in this ecosystem can negatively affect the different areas of your life. When one or two of your chakras are blocked, you'd experience health and mental issues.

There are many energy centers in your body, but there are seven major chakras that are located from the base of your spine to the top of your head.

Solar Plexus Chakra (Manipura)

This chakra is located in the upper abdomen or the stomach area, between the rib and the navel. This chakra governs your self-confidence. It is associated with different organs such as the spleen, liver, small intestine, and pancreas.

People with balanced solar plexus chakra has a childlike energy. They are open-minded, stress free, and they respect authority. They have a strong sense of community and team spirit. They also have integrity and a strong will. They're also practical and intellectual.

The governing element of this chakra is fire. When this chakra is unbalanced, you'll have "gut feelings" that could make you feel stressed or agitated. You'll also have poor memory and concentration.

If you need a quick confidence booster, you have to take time to balance this chakra. Balancing this chakra makes you feel centered in spirit, body, and mind. It also helps you get more connected with your intuition or gut feelings so that you may act accordingly and with confidence.

This chakra is associated with various gems and stones, including malachite, topaz, and orange calcite.

Root Chakra (Mooladhara)

The root chakra is the first chakra and its color is red. It is the most dense of all the chakras. Its element is earth and located at the base of the spine, right above your tailbone.

This chakra is associated with bladder, kidneys, hips, legs, and the vertebral column.

This chakra is associated with different gems and stones such as fire agate, black tourmaline, blood stone, hematite, and tiger's eye.

Sacral Chakra (Swadhisthana)

The sacral chakra is the second chakra. It is located below the navel and above your pelvic bone. Its color is orange and is associated with various organs, including the uterus, prostate, testes, ovaries, intestines, belly, lower sacrum, and bladder.

People with balanced sacral chakra are generally enthusiastic, happy, energetic, sporty, self-assured, and constructive. When this chakra is balanced, your body moves freely and easily. You also enjoy good health. You are motivated and focused in pursuing your personal goals.

When you have a balanced sacral chakra, you interact harmoniously with others and you have happy and mutually supportive relationships. You'll feel fulfilled and you do not feel any void.

This chakra governs your ability to feel pleasure and enjoyment. It also influences your sexuality, desire, and libido. When your sacral chakra is balanced, you'll feel like a sex goddess or god. You'd be sexually confident and you have a satisfying sex life.

This chakra is associated with various gems and stones, including the citrine, carnelian, coral, and moonstone.

Heart Chakra (Anahata)

The heart chakra is the fourth chakra. It is located at the center of the chest. It is the center of the chakra system and it governs one's immune system, lungs, thymus glands, heart, and blood circulation. It also governs our ability to give and receive unconditional love.

People with balanced heart chakra are compassionate and caring. They also have the ability to easily adapt to change. They are calm, friendly, fun, and cheerful.

But, people with overactive heart chakra are codependent. They tend to be too concerned on the needs of other people, to the point of neglecting their own emotional needs. They love indiscriminately. This could lead to abuse and unhappiness.

People with unbalanced chakras are apathetic, unforgiving, hopeless, detached, distrustful, and detached. They also experience physical symptoms such as pneumonia, asthma, respiratory problems, upper back pain, and premature aging.

This chakra is associated with various gems and stones, including green jasper, emerald, jade, green tourmaline, rhonodite, green moldavite, dipotase, peridot, moss agate, aventurine, and chrysoprase.

Throat Chakra (Visuddha)

This chakra, as the name suggests, is located at the throat. It is associated with self-expression, creativity, and truth. This chakra allows you to communicate your thoughts and feelings. Its color is blue and its governing element is air.

When this chakra is balanced, you can easily express what you feel. You can easily communicate your beliefs, ideas, and emotions. You're also really creative – you sing, draw, write poetry, or do woodworking.

When your throat chakra is imbalanced, you'll most likely engage in habitual lying. So, if you have a habit of lying to yourself and others and you have a hard time separating lies from the truth, you may have an unbalanced throat chakra.

This chakra is associated with various gems and crystals including aquamarine, turquoise, lapis lazuli, and sodalite.

Third Eye Chakra (Ajna)

This chakra is located on the forehead, between the eyes. Its color is indigo and it represents our ability to see the big picture and make sound decisions.

When this chakra is not balanced, you easily feel stressed and your judgement is often clouded. You also have a hard time organizing your thoughts or making a practical decision.

This chakra is associated with different crystals and precious stones such as purple amethyst, tanzanite, danburite, satyaloka quartz, herderite, scolecite, petalite, and phenacite.

Crown Chakra (Sahasrara)

This chakra is located at the top of your head. It represents your spirituality and it allows you to experience pure bliss. It represents universal wisdom, inner peace, clarity, unity, and enlightenment. Its color is purple and its governing element is ether or space.

When this chakra is balanced, you have the ability to understand things in a much wider context. You feel that you are always in the right place at just the right time. You'll also feel empowered and joyful.

When this chakra is not balanced, you'd experience a number of psychological and physical issues such as depression, confusion, mental disconnection, schizophrenia, epilepsy, light sensitivity, headaches, and neurological disorders. Crown chakra imbalance also causes you to become selfish, greedy, materialistic, and domineering. So, if you're too bossy or you find joy in shopping at high end department stores, you may have an unbalanced crown chakra.

This chakra is associated with a number of crystals such as rainbow quartz, amethyst, black merlinite, beta quartz, hyalite opal, nirvana quartz, clear quartz, howlite, rutilated quartz, and sugilite.

The root chakra, solar plexus chakra, sacral chakra, heart chakra, throat chakra, third eye chakra, and the crown chakra are the seven major chakras. But, some chakra systems actually have 12 chakras, which include the earth star chakra, navel chakra, causal chakra, soul star chakra, and stellar gateway.

Soul Star

The eighth chakra is called the soul star chakra. This chakra cleanses and heals your lower body. It is located around eighteen inches above the crown chakra. This chakra is known as the seat of the soul. This chakra governs your life purpose.

Earth Chakra

The earth chakra is the ninth chakra. It is located one foot below the ground. This chakra keeps you connected to the earth. It is the center of a powerful force called Kundalini.

Solar Chakra

This is the tenth chakra. This chakra attaches you to the angels that dwell in the sun. This chakra plays an important role in spiritual evolution.

Galactic Chakra

This chakra is hooked up from the palm of your hand and it is linked into the galactic system.

So, if you want to get the best out of life, you should make an effort to clear your energy centers and make sure that they are functioning correctly.

How Chakras Work

We all have a physical body and we also have an energy body. Our energy body contains our auras and meridian lines. Auras are non-physical energy fields that surround a person. Your aura reveals your thoughts, dreams, and feelings. The colors of your aura may vary and they are usually seen by people who have special training in the healing arts.

A meridian line, on the other hand, is a path where the life energy called "qi" or "chi" passes through. It is a typically used in Chinese medicine. If you go to an acupuncturist or a spiritual healer, you'll hear these terms often.

When you cut the body open, you won't see these auras and meridian lines, but you know that they are there. When you are familiar with auras, you'd know that they are affected by certain vibrations – good or bad. So, if you get a good vibe or bad vibe from someone, you may be feeling his aura. You get certain feelings when you talk with someone because these vibrations are contained in their energy.

Like the auras and meridian lines, the chakras are part of the body's energy anatomy. They operate like a ball of energy and they spin like a wheel to distribute your energy evenly throughout your body.

You can't see these chakras through an X-ray because they are not part of the physical body. They are part of our consciousness and they interact with the physical body through the different organs in the body. Each chakra is associated with one endocrine gland and a group of nerves called plexus.

As mentioned in the earlier chapter, there are seven major chakras or energy centers. Are some chakras more important than others? The answer is no. All chakras are equally important. To live a good life, you should balance all the chakras in your body.

The grounding function of the root chakra is just as important as the spiritual function of the crown chakra and the transcendent quality of the heart chakra.

To optimize your mental and bodily functions, you have to balance all your chakras and address your basic, relational, creative, safety, belongingness, and self-actualization needs.

The Chakras and Your Physical Body

We are all made of pure energy. So, if your energy centers are blocked, you'll experience various illnesses. When one or two of your chakras are not spinning, the energy is not evenly distributed throughout your body, resulting to some of organs may not functioning well.

For example, your heart chakra is in your chest area and it covers the heart, and the respiratory system. So, if your heart chakra is not spinning, you'll experience heart and circulation problems. You are also susceptible to respiratory diseases and allergies.

The throat chakra governs the throat and mouth area of your body. So, if it's not functioning well, you'll experience mouth ulcers, sore throats, and thyroid problems.

Many Western medical practitioners do not believe this, but your chakras can affect your body functions. Balanced chakras can optimize your health and vitality while unbalanced chakras can wreak havoc in your life.

Chakras and Emotions

Chakras do not only represent your physical body, but also your emotions and parts of your consciousness. When there is tension in your consciousness, you'll feel it in the chakra that's linked to that part of your consciousness.

For example, if your boyfriend leaves you, you'll feel the pain in your heart or chest area. You'll feel like you can't breathe. When you are nervous about something, your bladder becomes weak and your legs tremble.

When the tension persists, it can result to physical symptoms.

The Chakras and The Quality of Life

The chakras do not only affect your physical body, they also affect your mental health and the overall quality of your life. So, if one part of your life seems off or something in your life is not working, then one of your chakras may be blocked.

When one or two of your chakras are blocked, some parts of your life may be doing well while other parts of your life may not be doing well at all. For example, your career may be doing well, but you have difficulty maintaining healthy relationships.

 If you are a spiritual, kind, and compassionate person, but you have a hard time paying your bills, you may also have blocked chakras.

When your chakras are not functioning the way they should, you feel there is an imbalance. Your subconscious tells you that something is amiss.

The chakras represent who you are – your intellect, emotions, creativity, spirituality, sexuality, careers, principles, and your belief system. So, if your chakras are not balanced, you'll lose sight of one part of your life. You'll likely develop psychological problems such as depression, anxiety, delusions, and even nervous breakdown.

What Causes Chakra Blockages

Chakra blockages are caused by several factors – *belief system, career, living situation, financial situation and relationships.* Traumatic experiences such as abuse, accident, and loss of a loved one may also cause chakra blockages. Negative emotions such as anxiety, anger, stress, and fear may also put your chakras out of balance.

For example, being physically and emotionally abused by a former partner may cause heart chakra imbalance. You might have ended up closing yourself out to potential romantic partners. You may also tend to feel empty most of the time.

Your root chakra represents the foundation of your being. So, if your parents do not have enough money when you were growing up and they failed to provide enough for you, you'll most likely experience root chakra blockage. You may constantly fear that you do not have enough. You may also constantly worry about money.

Opening and Closing the Chakras

The opening and closing of your chakras work a lot like an energetic defense system. When you experience something traumatic or negative, the associated chakra will close itself to keep the negative energy out. If you are clinging to low frequency feelings such as anger, guilt, or blame, you'll experience chakra blockage.

Holding on to the following low frequency emotions for a long period can cause chakra blockage:

- Anger
- Pain
- Resentment
- Jealousy
- Covert hostility
- Grief
- Apathy
- Hopelessness
- Sadness
- Apathy
- Regret
- Pessimism
- Worry

- Blame
- Discouragement
- Shame
- Powerlessness
- Depression
- Disappointment
- Frustration
- Despair
- Guilt

The following positive or high frequency emotions can raise your vibrations and help open your chakras:

- Love
- Joy
- Acceptance
- Eagerness
- Optimism
- Passion
- Hopefulness
- Contentment
- Faith
- Belief

So, to keep your chakras balanced, you must let go of egoism. You must choose to act with love. You should also consider trying various chakra healing tools which will be discussed later in this book.

Chakras and Empaths

Many people have open chakras. These people are called empaths. They are highly sensitive people. They easily pick up other people's energy so they find public places overwhelming. They also know when someone is not being honest with them. They are creative and they have a strong need for solitude. They feel weak when they are exposed to toxic people.

Empaths should keep their chakras guarded and balanced. They should carry protective stones such as rose quartz, black tourmaline, amethyst, and malachite. These stones help balance emotions and remove anxieties and negative energy.

Symptoms of blockage

Chakra blockage can wreak havoc in your life. It can lead to weight fluctuations, health problems, financial problems, and relationship problems. It can lead to crippling phobias and physical issues. It can also lead to depression, anxiety, and other mental health issues.

When your chakras are blocked, you'd feel that something in your life is off. You'd have persistent worries, such as money problems, career difficulties, and fear of intimacy. If you feel that your finances, relationships, career, and everything else in your life is crumbling down, it's time to act.

Here's a guide that can help you determine if one or two of your chakras are blocked.

Crown Chakra Blockage

Your crown chakra is the gateway to wisdom and enlightenment. It connects you to the universe and everything in it. A blocked crown chakra can lead to spiritual connection, it can also lead to a number of symptoms including:

- Loneliness
- Lack of direction
- Inability to build a genuine connection with others
- Inability to set and maintain goals
- Nerve pain
- Learning difficulties
- Indecisiveness
- Lack of inspiration and joy
- Confusion
- Over intellectualism
- Dominance
- Nightmares
- Epilepsy
- Brain tumors
- Amnesia
- Delusions

Having an underactive crown chakra leads to confusion, spiritual addiction, catatonia, and over intellectualism. This means that if you're a "know-it-all", your chakra may be spinning too slowly.

Overactive crown chakra leads to dominance, depression, greed, headaches, and disconnection from reality. This is the reason why you should make sure that your crown chakra is balanced. There are many ways to do this, which we will discuss in the later chapters.

You can also say the following affirmations to help balance your crown chakra:

- I am complete.
- I am one with the Divine Energy.
- I am a spiritual being.
- I have faith in God.
- I believe.
- I go beyond my limiting beliefs.
- I am aligned with the Divine Energy.
- I am wise.
- I am open to questions
- I trust God.
- I understand.
- I am open to enlightenment.
- I am open for pure bliss.
- My consciousness is growing and expanding.
- God's love heals me.

- I let my fantasy run free.
- I am open minded.
- I accept myself totally.
- I am enlightened.
- I feel pure joy.

Root Chakra Blockage

The Muladhara chakra governs your ability to connect with the world. This chakra is extremely sensitive. This chakra represents security and stability.

When this chakra is blocked, you'd experience the following symptoms:

- Kidney infections
- Tumors in the rectal area
- Reproductive health issues
- Laziness
- Addictive behavior
- Anemia
- Circulatory issues
- Bladder irritations
- Anxiety
- Depression
- Low self esteem
- Leg pain
- Lower back pain
- Fear of change
- Materialism
- Anxiety attacks
- Lack of energy and motivation
- Insecurities

When you feel a lot of these symptoms, take time to sit down, breathe, and say these affirmations:

- I am grounded.
- I am safe.
- I am powerful.
- I am wealthy.
- I have enough.
- I am brave.
- I have enough.
- I am centered.
- I trust myself.
- I am open to possibilities.
- I am safe.
- I am loved.
- I am not afraid to change
- I am not afraid to trust people.
- I nurture my body with clean water, food, exercise, and water.

Sacral Chakra

Your sacral chakra is the center of your feelings and emotions. It is also the center of your sexuality and creativity. When your sacral chakra is balanced, you radiate sincere friendliness and warmth, without being too clingy. When you have a balanced sacral chakra, you have strong intuition, energy, and a strong zest for life. You're also compassionate and emotionally stable.

But when this chakra is off, you'll also feel that something's not right in your life. It could lead to various symptoms such as:

- Guilt
- Lack of motivation
- Infertility issues
- Low back pain
- Low libido
- Inability to orgasm
- Depression
- Low self-esteem
- Jealousy
- Detachment
- Fear
- Lack of vitality
- Fear of change
- Diabetes
- Sexual dysfunction

- Lack of flexibility
- Diarrhea
- Weight loss
- Loss of appetite
- Chameleon personality
- Depression
- Menstrual issues
- Lack of focus
- Poor boundaries
- Bipolar mood swings
- Immobilized by fear
- Aloofness

When your sacral chakra spins too fast, you often experience jealousy, mood swings, and sexual addictions. You often consider people as sex objects and you may be overly dramatic. If your sacral chakra is underactive, you may have digestive disorders and sexual issues. You may be oversensitive and shy.

If you're overly shy or you've been acting like a drama queen lately, then you should say the following affirmations daily:

- I am confident.
- I am comfortable with my sexuality.
- I accept myself.
- I am at peace.
- I am radiant.

- I listen to my own truth.
- I respect my emotions.
- I have the capability to provide for my own needs.
- I trust my instinct.
- My sexuality is sacred.
- I am enough.
- I am graceful.
- I am creative.
- I am grateful for everything in my life.
- The universe is filled with beauty.

Solar Plexus Chakra

When your solar plexus is balanced, you have complete control over your thoughts and emotions. Your small mind or ego won't influence your actions. You fully accept your place in the universe. You love and appreciate yourself and others. You can also easily see the uniqueness and importance of the people around you.

When this chakra is balanced, you have a healthy self-esteem. You have good relationships.

If this chakra is unbalanced, you're overly critical and judgmental. You'll easily find fault in others. You may be demanding and may have extreme emotional problems. You may be rigid and stubborn. You are also more likely to engage in a codependent relationship. You'll also experience the following symptoms:

- Diabetes
- Binge eating
- Constipation
- Lack of self control
- Gallstones
- Hepatitis
- Inability to lead others
- Stomach ulcers
- Self-esteem issues
- Allergies

- Pancreatitis
- Reflux problems
- Obesity
- Inability to reach goals
- Stomach ulcers
- Growing addiction

When your solar plexus chakra is not balanced, you can say the following affirmations:

- I am strong and powerful.
- I am empowered.
- I make my own choices.
- I treat myself respectfully.
- I trust myself.
- I am worthy of love and kindness.
- I am authentic.
- I direct my own life.
- I am at peace with myself.
- I am responsible for my life.
- I release my desires and appetite to the universe.
- I accept my responsibilities.
- I make my own choices.
- I am successful.
- I am in control.

You can also do yoga, color therapy, and other chakra balancing tools that we will discuss later in this book.

Blocked Heart Chakra

Holding a grudge or a traumatic event may block your heart chakra. Repressed feelings can also negatively affect the function of your heart chakra and can lead to:

- Heartlessness
- Fear of getting hurt
- Loneliness
- Social anxiety
- Shyness
- Holding grudges
- Inability to give or receive freely
- Fear and suspicion in romantic relationships and friendships
- You are extremely self-centered.
- You feel unworthy of love.
- You feel embarrassed of your failures.
- You easily lose patience.
- You have difficulty breathing and you have allergies.
- You have heart and lung issues.
- You may experience insomnia.

When you have an overactive heart chakra, you are unable to say no to others. You try your best to please others and you are desperate for other people's love and appreciation.

When you have an underactive chakra, you feel like you're cold, shy, and resentful.

The heart chakra controls most of your emotions. So, if you want to achieve emotional stability, it is important to keep this chakra balanced. If your heart chakra is not working well, you can say these affirmations:

- Love is all there is.
- I am worthy of love and respect.
- I love myself just as I am.
- I forgive myself and I forgive others.
- I trust in the power of love.
- My heart is filled with love.
- I open my heart to unconditional love.
- I love my life.
- I am compassionate.
- I openly receive love.
- I am not afraid to love.
- I am compassionate and forgiving.
- I am grateful.
- I embrace love.
- I open my heart to love.

These affirmations will help heal emotional wounds. If you have problems giving and receiving love, say these affirmations in the morning after you wake up and at night before you fall asleep.

Throat Chakra

As mentioned earlier, this chakra governs our ability to tell the truth. So, habitual lying is not just a character flaw, it is also a symptom of blocked throat chakra.

Throat chakra blockage has also a number of other emotional and physical symptoms such as:

- Extreme shyness
- Social anxiety
- Inability to express thoughts
- Inconsistency in actions and speech
- Social anxiety
- Detachment
- Stubbornness
- Inhibited creativity
- Detachment
- Chronic sore throat
- Laryngitis
- Frequent headaches
- Mouth ulcers
- Thyroid problems
- Neck pain
- Hoarseness

People with blocked throat chakra are deceptive, manipulative, domineering, anxious, and insecure. So, if you're constantly insecure or envious, take time to say the following affirmations:

- I have a voice.
- My opinions matter.
- I speak the truth.
- I uphold the truth.
- I am free of all delusions
- I claim my voice.
- I am speaking my personal truth.
- I let go of the chains that are holding me back.
- I have a beautiful voice.
- I am not afraid to speak my feelings.
- I listen to others with others.
- I am content and truthful.
- I value honesty.
- **Important.**
- I am not afraid to speak up.

Third Eye Chakra Blockage

Third eye chakra blockage can wreak havoc to your health. It could disrupt your day and it could lead to serious mental issues. It's normal to feel crazy on some days. But, if you're feeling crazy too often, then you may have a blocked third eye chakra.

This chakra governs your psychic abilities and intuition. So, if you feel that your intuition is out of whack or you get deceived easily, you may be experiencing third eye chakra blockage.

If your third eye chakra is blocked, you'll experience these symptoms:

- Poor vision
- Seizure
- Migraines
- Sciatica
- Inability to focus
- Oversensitivity
- Delusions
- Depression
- Paranoia
- Anxiety
- Fear of success
- Lack of clarity
- Paranoia

- Cognitive problems
- Psychotic behavior
- Severe retardation
- Lack of discipline
- Pride

If your third eye chakra spins too fast, you're proud, dominant, manipulative, and you may be living in a fantasy world. If it spins too slow, you're often confused, undisciplined, afraid of success, oversensitive, and unable to focus.

So, if you have an imaginary fiancé or you're experiencing other third eye chakra blockage, then you must take action by saying these affirmations:

- I see clearly.
- I have a strong intuition.
- I have an open sixth sense.
- I am important.
- I am intelligent.
- I am open.
- I am ready to see the truth.
- I am wise.
- I trust my intuition.
- I forgive myself for my past mistakes.
- I accept myself.
- I am open to bliss and inspiration.

- I am at peace.
- All is well.
- I release my past.

When you feel that something is off in your life, one or two of your chakras may be unbalanced. Later on in this book, you'll learn tips on how to heal and balance your chakras.

Chapter 5: Yoga and Chakras

One of the most popular tools to use in order to help your chakras get back in line is to use yoga. Tantric yoga is one of the best, but any type of yoga can really help and will ensure that you are able to get the results that you would like from blocked or damaged chakras. This chapter is going to take some time talking about tantric yoga since this one most closely relates to the chakras, but if you want to learn just a little beginning yoga to get started, this can do wonders for the chakras as well.

According to tantric yogis, yoga is able to help you to get some improvement to your chakras because it is going to help you experience some specific differences in your life. Because of this, you are able to feel the new changes that come from within you. A good way to see this is the chakras as a spinning wheel because they will involve a convergence of the energies, feelings, and thoughts that come together with their particular physical bodies. Whenever this does happen, you will learn to separate your emotions from reality, fear from confidence, and your aversions from your desires. Yoga will be able to get all of this back in order, and if there are some issues with a chakra being blocked, it will be able to unravel this so that you can reach that higher potential.

The best yoga poses for your chakras

Yoga is really easy to learn and you are going to fall in love with how great it is going to make your energy feel, even as a beginner. Spending just a few minutes on yoga each day is often enough to help you to get the energy back, and the balance that you need to feel amazingly in no time. Some of the best poses that you are able to work on for your chakras include:

- The Warrior I: this is a good pose to use when you need to have a better connection to the earth. It is going to give you a good foundation to the foot. The hips are going to get a good stretch for this pose, which can help to release some of the stale energy that is found in the root chakra.
- Bound Angle Pose: this is a good one to help open up the hips and will bring some attention to the pelvic region. Stretching this groin is going to help to release this tension and helps that chakra to work the way that it should.
- Navasana: this one is also called the Boat Pose and it is going to be used to stimulate your third chakra. This one is going to be located with your solar plexus and the Navasana is going to activate the fire

67

from Manipura while also helping us to connect with our own center.

- Camel pose: this one is great for opening up the heart center. It is common for many people to protect their hearts while also closing them off to vulnerability, but this is going to limit the experiences that we have on a daily basis. When we use the Camel Pose to help us with our heart chakra, we are exposing our hearts so that we can invite and give out more love.

- Fish Pose: this is a good one to release the throat chakra. When we take the time to stretch out the throat, it is going to make it easier to express ourselves freely through our own unique voices, rather than relying on others to make decisions all the time for us.

- Child's pose: this is a really simple pose, but it is going to connect the third eye right to the floor and will help to stimulate the intuition center in our bodies. By activating and bringing some awareness to this chakra, we are going to have a better access to our own great inner wisdom. You can also stack the first under the third eye while doing this pose to help bring out some more stimulation.

- Headstand: this one is a bit harder to do for a lot of people, but when you do, it is going to activate the crown chakra because it places some pressure on the top of your head. This is your gateway to universal consciousness and when we stimulate it, we are bringing attention to this area, making it easier to connect to the higher self that we should be.

To get the most out of these moves, it is a good idea to do a sequence of them and make that your workout. Holding each pose for about ten deep breaths before moving on can help you to hold them long enough to get the stretch that you need before moving on to the next move. It is also recommended that you would go through this list about two or three times, maybe more if the issues are really bad with some of your chakras. This is just a seven move sequence, so it doesn't take too much of your time and can really make you feel better in no time.

Of course, if you are short on time and just feel like one or two of the chakras are giving you some trouble, it is also possible to just pick out from these positions above and get the one that you think will work the best for you. A minute or so in each pose can do wonders for opening up that chakra and helping it to feel better than before. It is important to listen to your body and learn when it needs you to make some changes or to understand when one of the chakras is not working the way that you would like.

The chakras and yoga were developed along the same school of thought, and in the same tradition many years ago, which is why many times it is expected that you would work on yoga a bit if you would like to see your chakras clear up. Yoga is a pretty simple exercise and whether you make this part of your meditation and rest each day or use it after some tough workouts, it is still going to give you the benefits that you are looking for. Try out a few of these poses on occasion, at least, and you will love the big difference that it can make for your overall health.

Chapter 6: How to awaken the Chakras

It takes work to keep all your chakra points opened and aligned especially since they are not going to activate automatically. There are exercises, both physical and breathing, used for each chakra in order to "wake" them up, so to speak.

Root Chakra

Stand in a comfortable position with your feet hip-width apart. Rotate your hips from right-to-left 50 times, while breathing deeply.

Repeat the step above, only this time you'll move your hips from left-to-right.

Solar Plexus / Navel Chakra

Suck your stomach in as far as you can while breathing deeply 50 times. However, don't suck in your stomach **too** far. It is important that you experience no pain while performing this exercise.

Heart Chakra

Stretch your arms from side-to-side and in a circular motion, while breathing deeply 49 times. Then, move your arms in an up-and-down motion, while taking 3 breaths.

Throat Chakra

Bend your head down so that you're facing the ground and roll it to the left, to the back and now forward. With each head roll, breathe deeply 7 times.

Third Eye Chakra

Raise your eyebrows and take 49 deep breaths. Then close your eyes and focus on the breathing.

Crown Chakra

Lift up your arms above your head and take 7 breaths.

All humans absorb energy from others, both positive and negative. If you absorb negative energy, then you, in turn, will become bitterly angry, or even ill. These feelings may be the results of unbalanced chakras, but it is solely up to **you** to get your feelings under control.

To restore balance to your chakra points, create for yourself a private space free of noise and distractions. Surround yourself with natural elements or your gemstones and crystals. You should also imagine color and light auras surrounding you.

To connect with your spirit guide, say phrases of assurance and prayers. Remind yourself that you are free to express your true feelings and love and feel loved as your soul truly feels and desires. You are also completely free to live life the way you want, with no one stopping you.

Test your chakra points by waving your hand around each point to make sure each one is working.

Chapter 7: Tools to help with Chakras

Crystals

Crystals, when used properly, will also aid in strengthening your chakras, in addition to the guidelines given in the previous chapter. However, in order for them to work properly to their full potential, you have to place them directly at your chakra points. Here are the appropriate stones to use for each chakra and why:

Root Chakra

Use garnet, as the root chakra's color is red. It helps you keep connected with nature and the earth, and to lose the sense of materialism, particularly when it comes to things you don't really need or have any real use for. For example, do you really **need** that extra high-profile car in your garage, and eventually all it really does is sit in your garage, collecting dust and dirt? Remember that "keeping up with the Joneses" will **not** get you through life the way it's truly meant to be lived rather than just robotically going through the motions.

Sacral Chakra

Carnelian is the ideal stone for the sacral chakra in order to keep you in tune with human nature and connection to the world. Your creativity and ability to keep your emotions balanced are important as well. With this, you will always feel as if you have a purpose in this world.

Solar Plexus Chakra

Citrine helps keep the negative energies outside of you and away from you. This is another stone that helps aid in and maintains emotional balance in order to focus on not only accomplishing your goals but also doing so in an effective, meaningful way.

Heart Chakra

To keep your heart chakra healthy and balanced, your best bet is the green aventurine to maintain human connection and compassion, as well as to aid in controlling any angry or hostile feelings you may have. It also provides a humbling inside of you, enabling you to realize that **everyone** on this earth needs and is deserving of compassion and love.

Throat Chakra

Jolite helps you best with effective self-expression and open, honest communication. It also helps you determine what works and doesn't work for you, be it physically, spiritually and emotionally. For example, if someone offers you ice cream and you know you cannot have it because of dairy allergies, you can politely refuse and explain why you cannot have it, and when you're polite about it and truthfully explain why you had to refuse it, the less likely that person's feelings will be hurt. Also keep in mind that the best forms of creativity, be it through poetry, song or visual arts, always come from the creator's most **honest** thoughts and life experiences.

Third Eye Chakra

Think of the amethyst as a rather multi-purpose gemstone, but specifically for the maintenance of healthy third eye chakra, it helps you bring peace into your life and helps you deal with stressful events in a calmer, more constructive manner in order to keep in touch not just with the real, carnal world but also your spiritual self. It also helps you not to act or speak without thinking of the consequences or hurt it may cause to others.

Crown Chakra

The rainbow moonstone is as multi-purposeful as the chakra itself. As an actual rainbow contains many colors, the crown chakra is also responsible for aiding in other chakras, if opened and used properly.

This gemstone helps you keep connected and grounded in your own spirituality, and **not** to use it to inflate your ego and act and think as if you're "above" everyone else in this world because of it. Remember, there are different paths of life for different people.

These stones will be most effective and healing if you are in a completely quiet space free of distraction, especially from negative influences. You can hold the crystals above you and rotate them a few times. You will know that these stones are working if you feel any sort of odd sensations.

Mediation

You can sit or lie down for your meditation practices. As much as possible though, try the lotus position in yoga for chakra meditation. It's best known as the pose requiring the practitioner to cross legs while sitting on ground or floor.

One of the noteworthy things about the lotus position is that it helps keep your chakras aligned. When your energy centers are aligned, life energy flows faster from one chakra to another. It will be uncomfortable initially, like the majority of yoga poses. However, you'll be more flexible and more at ease through constant practice.

Steps:

1. Sit with your legs extended in front of you.

2. Bend your right knee. Hold your right foot and rest it on your upper left thigh with your right sole facing

upwards. Over time, you can do this without holding your right foot.

3. Take a deep breath and bend your left knee. Bring it over your lower right leg and let your left foot rest on your upper right leg with your left sole facing upwards.

4. Straighten your back. Keep your knees as close together as much as you can.

5. Now, put your palms together like in a praying position. Make sure your forearms are parallel to the floor. This is also called the jnana mudra. (Mudra refers to the position of your hands during meditation.)

6. Close your eyes. Reflect on your day. Recall the thoughts, emotions and behaviors you had earlier. Feel your chakras starting from the lowest to the highest.

7. Separate the good and bad things. Feed your chakras with the positivity from the good things that happened to you during the day.

8. Drive away the negativity by letting go of the things you can't control and thinking of ways to resolve what you can resolve.

9. Take deep breaths and embrace the positive energy into your chakras.

10. Finish your chakra meditation with an affirmation. Simply state what you're feeling or what you want to get.

Visualizing

As a chakra healing technique, visualization or mental imagery involves picturing life energy and chakras. Compared to chakra meditation, visualization puts less emphasis on your negative emotions and thoughts. It focuses more on the flow of life energy.

Steps:

1. Sit or lie down comfortably. You may also do the lotus position.

2. Close your eyes. Focus on your breathing. Feel your body relaxing from each breath you take.

3. Recite affirmations such as "I feel calm" and "I am ready to heal my chakras".

4. Next, concentrate on your crown chakra. Imagine a light above your head. Visualize it enter your body through your crown chakra. Imagine it fill the said chakra with renewed energy and warmth. The light signifies the life energy from the universe.

5. Feel the light wash away your negative thoughts. Imagine your crown chakra emit a bright purplish glow. Next, feel the warmth and glow from the crown chakra. Direct the life energy toward the third eye chakra.

6. Imagine the third brow chakra glow with a purplish-blue color. This signifies that the life energy from the crown chakra has flowed down. Feel how the flow stops for a while and how the life energy still lingers and empowers your third eye chakra. Feel the life energy clear your vision. Visualize your third brow chakra emit a bright indigo glow.

7. Next, imagine the light go down to your throat chakra. Visualize the chakra emit a dark blue glow. This entails that the chakra receives the life energy. Feel the life energy stay there. Feel how it clears and enhances your throat chakra. Embrace the confidence it gives. Imagine the throat chakra shine with bright blue glow.

8. Visualize the life energy flow down your heart chakra, causing it to emit a dark green glow. Feel the light unblock your centermost energy center by eliminating negative emotions. Afterwards, imagine the dark green glow of your heart chakra turn into vibrant green.

9. Feel the life energy go down to your solar plexus chakra. Imagine the said energy center with a muddy yellow glow. Let it reawaken and strengthen the energy in the said chakra. After accepting the new supply of life energy, visualize your solar plexus chakra emit a bright yellow glow.

10. Imagine the yellow glow flow down to the sacral chakra, turning the chakra's orange glow into a dull one. Feel the life energy eliminate your self-identity issues. Once done, visualize your sacral chakra's orange glow become brighter.

11. Shift the life energy from your sacral chakra down to your root chakra. Visualize the latter with a red-orange or brown glow. Next, imagine the light bids your insecurities and fears goodbye. Let the life energy linger for a few more minutes in your body.

12. Lastly, visualize the light go underneath the ground. Let the earth process it to create positive or neutral life energy.

Journaling

Journaling is dubbed as a mental exercise. It requires being mindful as you have to recall your actions, emotions and thoughts the day before. However, it doesn't usually cover awareness of your chakras' conditions. This activity will make you feel more connected and in control of your energy centers if you write about them as part of your regular journal entries.

Start your journal entry by contemplating on what chakras seem to be off when you woke up earlier. Next, reflect on what happened during the day. Describe the environment that you're in and discuss your thoughts, emotions and actions. Assess which among your chakras are experiencing problems as evident in the way you think, feel and behave.

Journaling with chakras in mind is advantageous to the seven main chakras. Through this activity, you can pinpoint which among your energy centers need some healing. You can avoid the factors that worsen the chakra's condition and carry out healing practices.

The activity also offers additional benefits for the third, fifth, sixth and seventh chakras. Remember how the solar plexus chakra helps you deal with major life changes. Journaling keeps you aware of causes and impact of such changes. Such awareness strengthens your control of your third chakra.

As for your throat chakra, the mere act of writing everyday enhances the way you communicate. It trains you to organize your thoughts. It also teaches you the value of backing up your statements. When you write a journal entry, you just don't discuss what you think, feel and do; you're supposed to tell why as well.

Journaling also helps you keep your thought processes in check. Your train of thoughts can either supply positivity or negativity to your third eye chakra and crown chakra. Being conscious of the way you think helps you avoid going the negative route.

To make journaling an effective way to assess your chakras' condition, do it before bedtime. If you find journaling every day a bit dull, bullet journaling or scrapbooking may fit you. Aside from writing, you can exercise your sketching, painting and collage-making skills in those activities.

Summary Conclusion

Learning about chakras is a spiritual journey that everyone should take at some point in life. The lessons you learn are useful and will help you change the course of your life. Mastery of your chakras is important in that it accords you an infinite understanding of your spirituality and its connection to the universe around you. What is interesting about chakras is that they are things we know about, but never pay attention to. Most of the time you go about your life like a blind person, unaware of the energy around you, or the energy you emit. Ever wondered why you keep attracting bad company while other people attract good company?

In Sanskrit, you attract similar energy to the one you emit. If you constantly give off negative vibes, you will attract negativity. Those who give off positive energies always have positivity around them. You want nothing but good things in your life. It is time for you to embrace your spirituality, learn about your chakras, and how they affect or control your life. From the first to the last chakra, so much happens in your life that you should learn about. In this book, we covered some of the common symptoms to look for, which will alert you when your chakra is blocked, and what to do. Apart from the emotional and spiritual symptoms, we have also addressed physical experiences that should warn you when something is not right with any of your chakras.

The exercises and routines recommended for balancing your chakras are easy to perform. Allow yourself a few minutes each day for this, and you can get your life back in line. To live and enjoy your life with all the happiness that the universe bestows upon you, the secret lies in a mastery of the seven chakras. Mastery means you understand what they do, and how they control your life.

This level of mastery will help you improve your relationships with people around you, your relationships with nature and the entire universe. Balanced chakras give you peace, not just with people around you, but more importantly, peace with yourself. After all, you cannot know how to love and care for others until you to learn how to do the same for yourself, and the value it holds in your life.

References

https://www.thedailymeditation.com/4-best-chakra-books-you-need-to-read-in-2018

https://www.mindbodygreen.com/0-91/The-7-Chakras-for-Beginners.html

https://en.wikipedia.org/wiki/Chakra

https://chopra.com/articles/what-is-a-chakra

https://www.yogajournal.com/practice/beginners-guide-chakras

Made in the USA
Columbia, SC
31 July 2021